Dancing through Space

Dr. Mae Jemison Soars to New Heights

Lydia Lukidis

illustrated by
Sawyer Cloud

ALBERT WHITMAN & COMPANY
CHICAGO, ILLINOIS

Mae's curiosity was as wide as the sky.

She spent her days questioning,

exploring,

learning.

She absolutely loved...

SCIENCE!

Mae could not sit still.

She spent her days jumping,

flipping,

rolling.

She absolutely loved…
DANCE!

Mae spotted science everywhere, from symmetry to gravity.

She had more questions than there were stars in space.

How do rockets fly? What's a black hole? Why can't we see the moon during the day?

Her parents encouraged her to find the answers herself, like a true scientist.

Mae spotted choreography everywhere, from birds soaring to waves swirling.

She had more dance moves than there were leaves on a tree.

She twirled and whirled! She put on dance shows at family gatherings!

Mae explored the possibilities of movement, like a true dancer.

In kindergarten, Mae's teacher asked the students what they wanted to be when they grew up.

Mae's arm shot up. "I want to be a scientist."

"Oh?" Her teacher's smile faded. "Don't you mean a nurse?"

Mae placed her hands firmly on her hips. "No! I want to be a scientist."

Mae didn't want to take piano lessons like her sister.

She wasn't interested in accordion or karate like her brother.

She begged her parents to let her take dance classes. "Please, please, pleeeasse! I really want to do it!"

Mae often visited the local planetarium with her family. She loved learning about space; it was part of science. Sinking into the cushions, she gazed up into the universe. The stars dipped and danced around her. She wondered what it would feel like to float among those stars. She raised her arms as if to catch them.

Mae pleaded for years until her mother finally registered her for dance class. She wanted to try it all. First, ballet. Then, a year later, modern dance.

Mae's eyes sparkled. She raised her arms as she soared through the air.

Once, Mae got a splinter stuck in her thumb. It got infected. Her finger throbbing, hot tears spilled down her cheeks. Driven by curiosity, she turned to her science books to learn how the body copes with infections.

Science gave her courage.

To get to Saturday morning ballet class, Mae had to take a train high off the ground. It was five times her height! Heart racing and palms sweating, she marched toward the train, not daring to look down.

Dance gave her determination.

After graduating high school with honors, Mae received a scholarship to attend Stanford University. She decided to focus her scientific studies on chemical engineering. Juggling a full course load, she often went to bed at midnight and woke up at 4:30 in the morning to continue studying.

Her mind became strong and sharp.

Between classes and after school, Mae explored different dance styles. She stomped through African dance, shimmied her way through jazz, and shuffled through Japanese dance.

Her body became strong and muscular.

The world of science was not welcoming. There weren't many women in Mae's classes, and certainly none who looked like her.

Some of her professors pretended she wasn't there or belittled her. And when she told one of her classmates she wanted to apply to be an astronaut, he laughed. "You mean like the guys who go to the moon? Give me a break."

The world of dance was demanding. Rehearsals were long and rigorous. Mae practiced complicated dance moves over and over again. Sweat dripped down her forehead as her breathing deepened. She focused and tried to remember the next move, then leapt into the air to do a grand jeté.

THUD!

After graduating from college, Mae wondered what to do next. Medicine was exciting!

It was yet another branch of science she was curious about. She wanted to learn more about the human body and how to cure disease.

Dance was energizing!

It was part of Mae's soul, and her body longed to express itself.

She felt pulled in two different directions, so she decided...

to study them both!

"You can always dance if you're a doctor, but you can't doctor
if you're a dancer," her mother said.

Mae pursued her studies in medicine. Meanwhile, she never
stopped dancing. With every flip and every jump, her confidence
blossomed.

After years of hard work and tireless studying, Mae graduated and earned the title of doctor. She spent her days caring for patients.

At night, she often gazed up at the sky, remembering her frequent visits to the planetarium when she was younger. She still dreamed of dancing through space and floating among the stars.

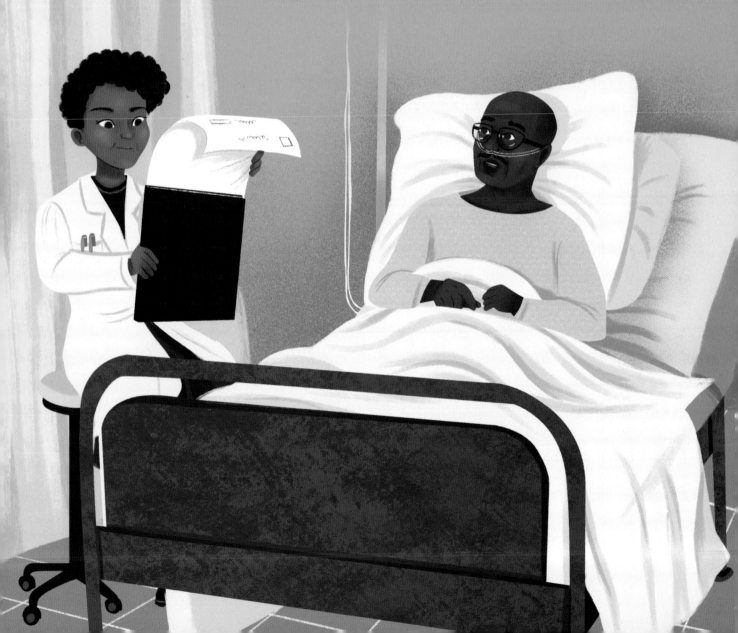

Soon after becoming a doctor, Mae applied to NASA's astronaut training program. Her background in science and medicine gave her the skills she needed to be an astronaut.

And then, a major disappointment: Mae didn't make it into the training program. NASA put it on hold because of the recent explosion of the Space Shuttle *Challenger*.

Mae's heart sank.

One day, Mae went to work as usual. She sat in her office taking notes, until—
RIIING!

It was NASA. The space program was back on, and they had chosen her out of more than two thousand applicants.

Mae's heart skipped a beat as she grinned from ear to ear.

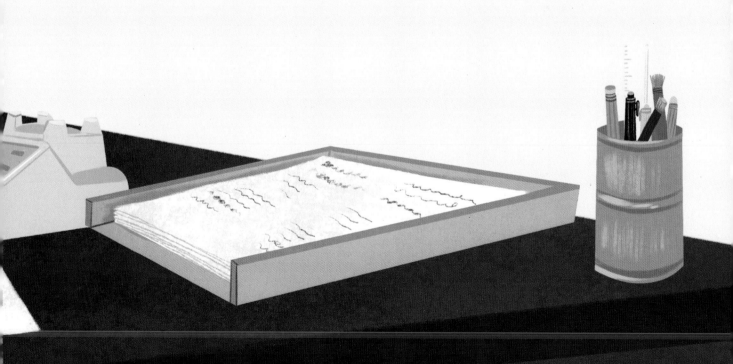

For over a year, Mae endured the challenges and demands of astronaut training. She floated in an antigravity tank and memorized hundreds of instructions for space station systems.

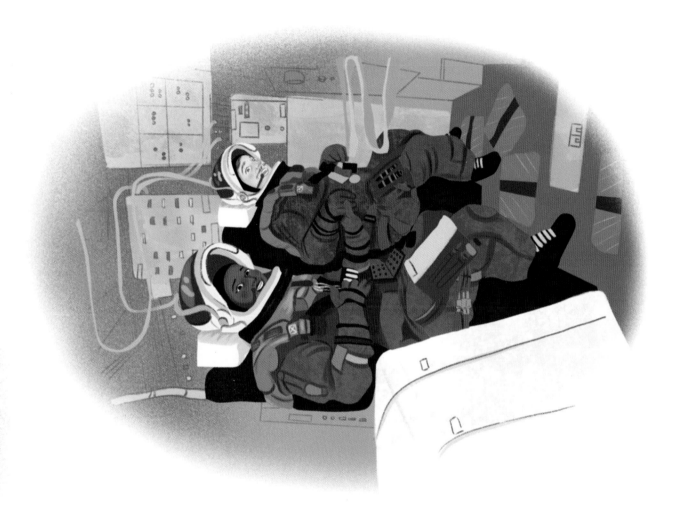

She also handled heavy equipment and practiced
countless flight simulations. The razor-sharp memory and
coordination she had developed as a dancer helped her
with these tough tasks.

On September 12, 1992, Mae blasted into space
aboard the Space Shuttle *Endeavour* along with six other
astronauts. Her heart soared as she catapulted into her
dreams. She was the first Black woman to fly into space.

The shuttle orbited the earth in a slow choreography,
and gravity melted away.

Mae spent the next seven days
flipping and rolling,
exploring and learning,

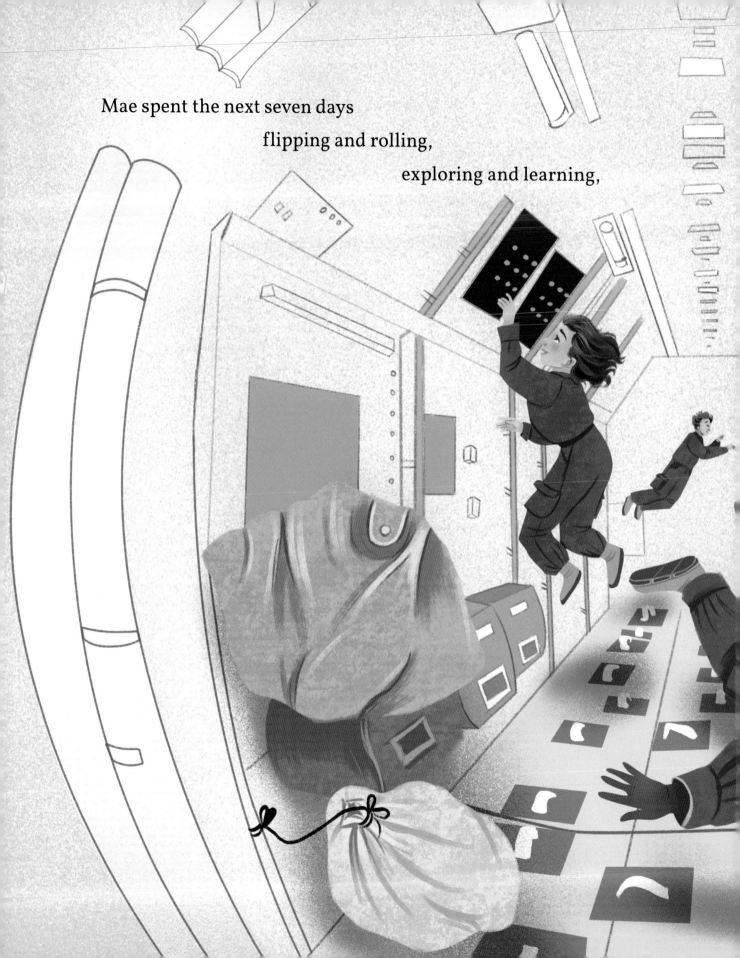

as she danced through space

and floated among the stars.

Author's Note

When I researched Dr. Mae Jemison's life, I was fascinated by her determination and perseverance. She always followed her dreams, no matter what obstacles lay in her way. It never occurred to her that she "couldn't" or "shouldn't" do certain things, like going to space.

The more I learned about Mae, the more I understood how important creativity is for her. Scientists tend to see life through the lens of reason and logic. While Mae uses science to explain the world, she also recognizes the value of art. Through her many different passions, she realized early on that science and art are not separate. They work together to give us a fuller understanding of who we are.

This concept mirrors my own life. Early on, I studied science and earned a degree in pure and applied science. When I went to university, I decided to leave that world behind to pursue art and literature. At the time, I saw science and art as separate fields. Today, my path has come full circle, and I understand that both worlds are, in fact, connected. I now use all the knowledge I gained when I studied science and pour it into my work as a writer. I love writing STEAM books that capture the magic around us, as well as the science in our everyday lives. My journey has taught me that we can be scientists and artists at the same time. That's why I felt so drawn to Mae's story and why I had to write this book.

"Many people do not see a connection between science and dance, but I consider them both to be expressions of the boundless creativity that people have to share with one another."

—*Dr. Mae Carol Jemison*

Dr. Mae Jemison accomplished many things. Her scientific curiosity opened the door to engineering, medicine, and astronomy. Her love of the arts also led her to study dance and choreography. But most of all, she's an agent of change.

1956: Mae Carol Jemison is born in Decatur, Alabama.

1959: Mae's family moves to Chicago, Illinois.

1973: Mae graduates from Morgan Park High School with honors.

1977: Mae receives degrees in chemical engineering and African and Afro-American studies from Stanford University.

1981: Mae graduates from Cornell University Medical College with a degree in medicine.

1983: Mae joins the Peace Corps and travels to West Africa, where she serves as a medical officer for two years.

1985: Inspired by astronaut Sally Ride and *Star Trek* actress Nichelle Nichols, Mae applies for admission to NASA's astronaut training program.

1986: The Space Shuttle Challenger explodes, and NASA puts the training program on hold.

1987: Mae reapplies and is accepted to NASA.

1992: Mae blasts into space aboard the Space Shuttle *Endeavour*. The mission lasts 7 days, 22 hours, 30 minutes, and 23 seconds. Mae and the crew conduct a variety of science experiments.

1993: Mae leaves NASA to pursue other dreams.

1993: Mae becomes a teacher at Dartmouth College and forms The Jemison Group, a technology design and consulting company.

2024: Retired, Mae lives in Houston, Texas. She continues to speak at conferences and travels to schools to talk about perseverance, the importance of pursuing one's dreams, and becoming an agent of change. She built a dance studio in her home and still enjoys dancing.

For my parents, Yorgo and Hrisula, who have consistently supported
my dreams throughout this wondrous journey.—LL

To Haikintana Astronomy, an association of passionate and astrophysicists
in Madagascar. Thank you for the love and dedication!—SC

Library of Congress Cataloging-in-Publication data is on file with the publisher.

Text copyright © 2024 by Lydia Lukidis
Illustrations copyright © 2024 by Albert Whitman & Company
Illustrations by Sawyer Cloud
First published in the United States of America in 2024 by Albert Whitman & Company
ISBN 978-0-8075-1458-0 (hardcover)
ISBN 978-0-8075-1459-7 (ebook)
Printed in China
10 9 8 7 6 5 4 3 2 1 WKT 28 27 26 25 24 23

Design by Shane Tolentino

For more information about Albert Whitman & Company,
visit our website at www.albertwhitman.com